George W. Bush: Our Forty-
Third President
Michael Burgan
AR B.L.: 6.7
Points: 1.0

George W. Bush

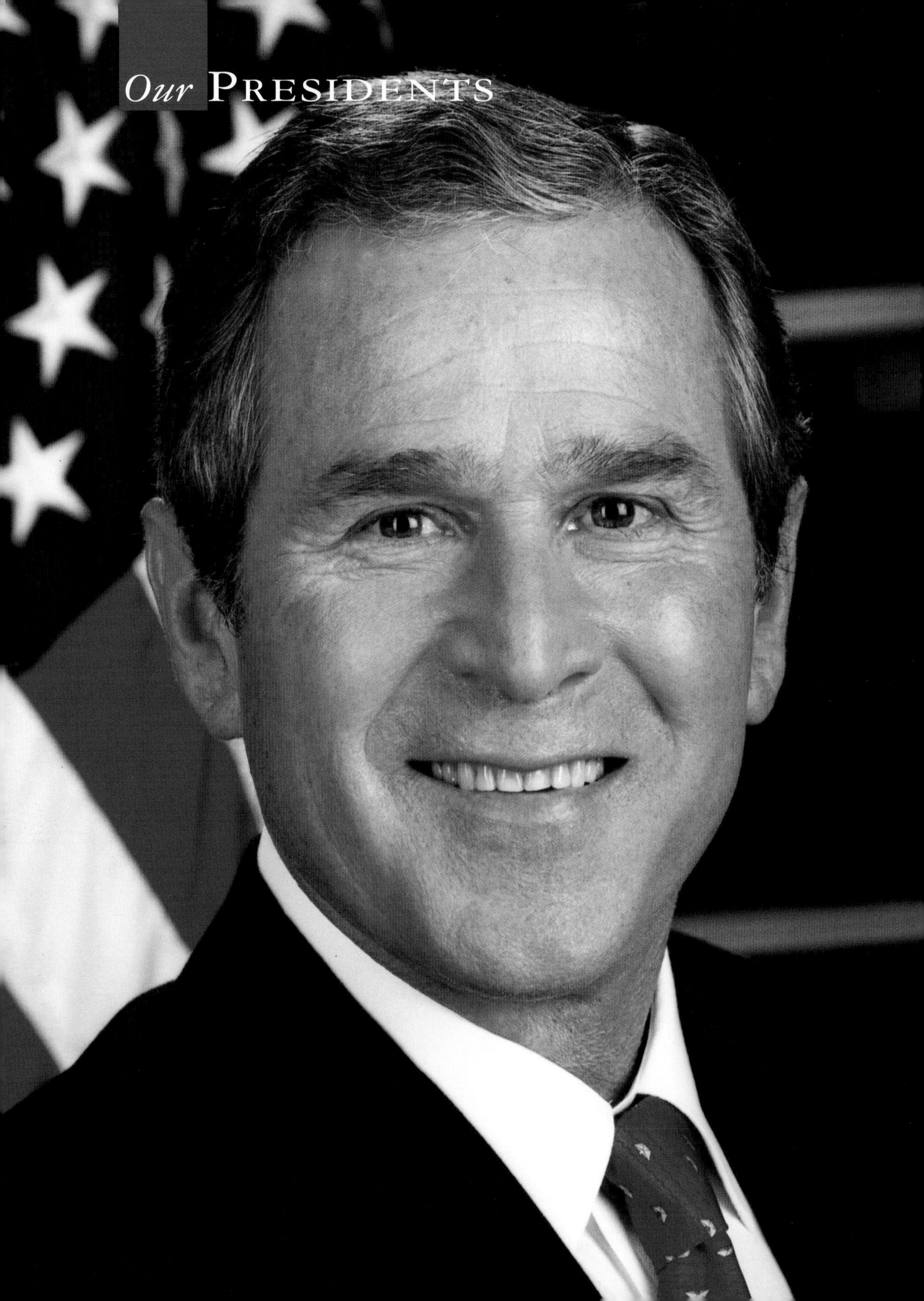

GEORGE W. *Bush*

OUR FORTY-THIRD PRESIDENT

By Michael Burgan

SPIRIT
of America®

The Child's World®
Chanhassen, Minnesota

9

GEORGE W. *Bush*

Published in the United States of America by The Child's World®
PO Box 326 • Chanhassen, MN 55317-0326 • 800-599-READ • www.childsworld.com

Acknowledgments

The Child's World®: Mary Berendes, Publishing Director

For Editorial Directions, Inc.: E. Russell Primm, Editorial Director; Pam Rosenberg, Editor, Katie Marsico, Associate Editor; Judith Shiffer, Assistant Editor; Matt Messbarger, Editorial Assistant; Susan Hindman, Copy Editor; Emily Dolbear, Proofreader; Olivia Nellums, Fact Checker; Tim Griffin/IndexServ, Indexer; Cian Loughlin O'Day, Photo Researcher, Linda S. Koutris, Photo Editor

The Design Lab: Kathleen Petelinsek, Design and Page Production

Photos

Cover/frontispiece: The White House Photo Office.

Interior: Corbis: 10 (Brooks Kraft), 13 (Tim Page), 20 (Alan Levenson), 24 (Bob Daemmrich); George Bush Presidential Library: 9, 12, 15, 16, 18, 21, 22; Getty Images: 33 (Time Life Pictures/Mai/Mai), 37 (Joe Raedle); Alain Nogues/Corbs Sygma: 38; Reuters/Corbis: 6, 26, 28, 29, 30, 35.

Library of Congress Cataloging-in-Publication Data

Burgan, Michael.
  George W. Bush : our forty-third president / by Michael Burgan.
    p. cm. — (Our presidents)
  Includes bibliographical references and index.
  ISBN 1-59296-494-X (lib. bound : alk. paper) 1. Bush, George W. (George Walker), 1946—Juvenile literature. 2. Presidents—United States—Biography—Juvenile literature. I. Title. II. Series.
  E903.B863 2006
  973.931'092—dc22   2004024066

Contents

Chapter ONE

A Family of Service

Terrorists flew planes into the Twin Towers of the World Trade Center on September 11, 2001. Nearly 3,000 people were killed that day.

ON THE MORNING OF SEPTEMBER 11, 2001, President George W. Bush sat in a Florida classroom. As he read to the students, he heard something that would change his presidency—and the United States—forever. An aide whispered in Bush's ear, "America is under attack."

Earlier in the morning, a jet plane had slammed into one of the famed Twin Towers. The towers, the tallest buildings in New York City, were part of the World Trade Center. Many people assumed the collision was an accident. But when another passenger plane crashed into the second tower, U.S. officials knew someone had **hijacked** the planes and was trying to kill American citizens. Before the morning was over, a third hijacked plane was flown into the Pentagon, and a fourth hijacked plane crashed in Pennsylvania. Nearly 3,000 Americans were killed that day. The most likely suspects were members of al-Qaeda, a **terrorist** group. "They had declared war on us, and I made up my mind at that moment that we were going to war," Bush later said.

Before the 2000 election, some Americans wondered if George W. Bush had enough experience with foreign affairs to be president. His only previous elected job was governor of Texas. But after the terrorist attacks, the public solidly supported George W. Bush. He quickly made plans to invade Afghanistan, where al-Qaeda was based. Bush also took steps to prevent more terrorist attacks in the United States. That policy included leading a **coalition** of countries whose troops invaded Iraq, a country which had helped terrorists in the past.

Bush promised he would do all he could to protect Americans. "I see dangers that exist,"

▶ George W. Bush's father, George H. W. Bush, served as the 41st U.S. president. The two Bushes were America's second father-and-son presidents. In 1796, John Adams was elected the second U.S. president, and his son John Quincy Adams was elected president 28 years later.

▶ Through his mother, Barbara, George W. Bush is related to Franklin Pierce, the 14th president of the United States. The Bushes also have distant family ties to Queen Elizabeth II of England.

the president said in 2004, "and it's important for us to deal with them." Later that year, a majority of American voters chose Bush to lead the United States for another four years. They thought he was the best person to keep the country safe during dangerous times.

Members of the Bush family have served in government since World War I (1914–1918). Samuel Prescott Bush, George W.'s great-grandfather, worked for a government agency that helped buy weapons for the U.S. military. His son Prescott Bush entered politics and was a U.S. senator from Connecticut for 10 years. Prescott's son George H. W. became active in politics in the 1960s and ran for president in 1988. His son George W. played an active role in that **campaign.** In many ways, the younger Bush often followed in his father's footsteps.

George H. W. Bush and his wife, Barbara Pierce Bush, lived in New Haven, Connecticut, when George W. was born on July 6, 1946. The elder Bush had served as a navy pilot during World War II (1939–1945). He was awarded the Distinguished Flying Cross for bravery in action. He then went to New Haven to study at Yale University, one of the top colleges in the United States.

In 1948, the Bushes moved to Texas. George H. W. got a job with a company that sold equipment to the oil industry. Oil had been a big business in Texas since it was first discovered in the state decades before. The Bush family had been successful in business for years, so George H.W. knew about the value of hard work. After a few years in Texas, he decided to start his own oil company.

George H. W., Barbara, and their young son settled in Midland, a small town in West Texas. George W. spent a large part of his childhood there before the Bushes moved to Houston. In 1949, the Bushes had a daughter named Robin. During the 1950s, George W.'s family grew to include his brothers Jeb, Neil, and Marvin, and his sister Dorothy. Robin, sadly, died of cancer before her fourth birthday. Relatives said George W. tried to cheer up his parents, who deeply felt the loss.

The George H. W. Bush family poses for a portrait in 1956. George W. stands farthest left, next to his mother.

Interesting Fact

▸ In a letter he wrote soon after moving to Texas, George H. W. described his young son. He said George W. "talks a blue streak" and "seems to be very happy wherever he is and is very good about amusing himself in the small yard we have."

In Texas, George W. attended both public and private schools. At 15, he entered Phillips Academy, a private high school in Andover, Massachusetts. His father had gone to the same school. A classmate recalled that George W. was "one of the cool guys" at the school. Although not a star baseball player like his father, George W. played on several sports teams. In class, he struggled at first, but as he later wrote, "I buckled down, worked hard, and learned a lot."

George W. Bush attended Phillips Academy, better known as Andover, where this picture of the young Bush (standing, second from left) and his teammates was taken in 1964.

In 1964, George W. graduated from Phillips Academy and planned to enter Yale University in the fall. During the summer, he returned to Texas, where George H. W. was beginning a campaign for the U.S. Senate. George's father, a member of the Republican Party, was mostly **conservative.** Most Texans at the time belonged to the Democratic Party. During the summer, the younger Bush rode a bus across the state, helping his father. George W. called his summer on the campaign a great experience, but his father lost the election in the fall.

During his four years at Yale, George W. studied history and enjoyed reading. He also briefly played on the baseball team and learned how to play rugby.

Those same years that George W. spent at Yale were sometimes difficult ones for the United States. African Americans were struggling to win legal equality with whites. Some people, especially in the South, resisted this effort. The country was also at war in Vietnam, and many college students protested the war. George W., like his father, was a conservative, and he opposed the protesters.

While serving in the Texas Air National Guard, George W. Bush flew fighter jets such as this F-102.

Interesting Facts

▶ At Yale, George W. Bush joined a social club called Skull and Bones. His father and grandfather had also been members. Skull and Bones is a secret society. Members meet in private and are not supposed to discuss the club and its activities with anyone who does not belong. Over the decades, many U.S. political and business leaders have been members of Skull and Bones.

▶ While George W. Bush was at Yale, his father won his first major political campaign and was elected to the U.S. House of Representatives.

He later called the mid-1960s "a confusing and disturbing time."

When George W. Bush left Yale in 1968, he joined the Texas Air National Guard. Some members of the Guard fought in Vietnam, but many, including Bush, remained in the United States. George W. spent most of the next two years learning how to fly fighter jets. After 1970, Bush served part-time in the National Guard, while he worked for several Republican **candidates** running for various offices statewide.

THE VIETNAM WAR SHARPLY DIVIDED AMERICANS. THE WAR STARTED DURING the 1950s. The North Vietnamese **Communists** and a group of South Vietnamese insurgents, people who opposed their government, wanted national reunification, a united Vietnam. With help from the insurgents, Communists from North Vietnam tried to take over South Vietnam. U.S. leaders opposed the spread of communism and sent aid and military advisers to the south. By 1965, U.S. combat troops were also in Vietnam. U.S. leaders believed if they did not stop the North Vietnamese and South Vietnamese insurgents, then other countries in the region would come under Communist rule.

Some opponents of the war, however, disliked South Vietnam's government. Its leaders did not allow free elections, and they stole aid money sent by the United States. The war protesters said the United States should not support such leaders, or send U.S. troops into battle over issues that did not directly affect the United States. During the war, many young men did not want to be **drafted.** Some fled to Canada. Others joined the military by going into the National Guard. While some National Guardsmen went on to serve in Vietnam, Bush did not.

Finding a Path

▶ While living in Houston in 1973, George W. Bush worked for a nonprofit group called Project PULL. He helped poor, young boys stay out of trouble.

GEORGE W. BUSH ENJOYED WORKING ON political campaigns more than he liked his first full-time job. In 1971, he began working for a Texas company that raised and produced food for farm animals. Bush called the position a "stupid coat-and-tie job" and left after one year. For a time in 1972, he thought about running for the Texas **legislature,** but he decided he wanted to gain more experience before entering politics.

By this time, George H. W. Bush was the U.S. **ambassador** to the **United Nations.** In that role, he met with ambassadors from around the world and tried to win support for U.S. policies. U.S. president Richard Nixon then asked the elder Bush to run the Republican Party. George H. W. Bush became one of the most important party members in the country.

Although he was drawn to politics, George W. also thought about someday running his own company. In 1973, he entered Harvard University to study for an advanced degree in business. Bush was now a more serious student than he had been in high school and college, and he enjoyed his classwork. When he graduated in 1975, he returned to Texas to enter the oil business.

Bush's first job was researching land records. He learned who owned the rights to valuable resources, such as oil or minerals, that might lie beneath a plot of land. Eventually, he bought and sold **leases** for these resources and then started drilling oil wells. The first one he drilled, he later wrote, was "a dry hole." But Bush kept trying and finally found oil. The oil business fascinated him. He knew, he later wrote, "that if I worked hard and hustled I could make a living."

George H. W. Bush served as the U.S. ambassador to the United Nations in 1971–1972.

Interesting Fact

▸ During George W. Bush's time at Harvard, his father became the U.S. ambassador to China. George W. briefly visited his parents there. Later, the elder Bush served as the head of the Central Intelligence Agency (CIA), the major U.S. spy agency.

15

George and Laura Bush were married on November 5, 1977, in Midland, Texas.

Bush did work hard and became successful. But he didn't lose his interest in politics. In 1977, he decided to run for the U.S. Congress. That same year, he met Laura Welch, a school librarian in Houston. The two quickly fell in love and married in November. With his campaign under way, Bush did not have time for a honeymoon. His first task was to beat other Republicans to win the party's **nomination.** He succeeded, and in the fall of 1978, he ran against the Democratic candidate.

The part of West Texas that Bush wanted

to represent was conservative, like Bush himself. But many of the voters distrusted people who were not from the region. Even though Bush had spent many years in Texas, some thought he was an outsider because his family had strong ties to the East. Some Texans also believed he was trying to use his father's reputation for his own gain.

That fall, Bush lost the race for Congress. "I put up a good fight," he later wrote. "I worked hard and enjoyed the campaign." Bush changed his focus to business, while his father reentered politics.

In 1980, George H. W. Bush ran for the Republican presidential nomination. He lost to Ronald Reagan, but Reagan then chose Bush as his vice presidential candidate. The younger Bush, his brothers, and his sister all worked for their father and Reagan during the campaign. In November, the Reagan-Bush team won the election. George W.'s father was now, as the saying goes, just "a heartbeat away" from the presidency.

For the next several years, George W. continued his work at Arbusto Energy, which he later renamed Bush Exploration.

George W. Bush walks up the South Lawn drive of the White House with his father in 1992.

At first, Bush did well in the oil business, but prices for oil began to fall in the mid-1980s. This made it hard for oil companies to earn money. Arbusto Energy merged with another oil company, Spectrum 7, and Bush became chairman. Spectrum 7 was later bought by another company.

Meanwhile, George H. W. Bush was achieving much success in politics. In 1984, Bush and Reagan were reelected. Soon after, the Bush family began preparing for George H. W.'s run in the 1988 presidential race. George W. played a major role in that campaign, helping his father win the support of conservative Christian voters. Conservative Christians, believe in traditional family values, prayer in schools, and the right to life. George

W. Bush convinced many of these voters that his father would support their political interests.

During the campaign, he also defended his father from public attacks by reporters and Democrats. "I earned and deserved a reputation for being feisty and tough, sometimes too tough," George W. later wrote.

In November 1988, George H. W. Bush won the presidency. Just before the new president and his wife settled into the White House, George W. moved into a new home in Dallas. Some journalists suggested he was thinking about running for governor in Texas. But in private, some Republicans in the state felt it was too soon for him to run for office. One Republican leader told him he needed "to go out in the world and do something."

Bush took that advice, and in 1989 he started a new business venture. He became a part owner of the Texas Rangers baseball team. Now he could combine his lifelong love of baseball with his business experience. As part owner, Bush attended games and met the players. He also represented the other owners in public. His new job helped voters see that Bush was more than just the president's son.

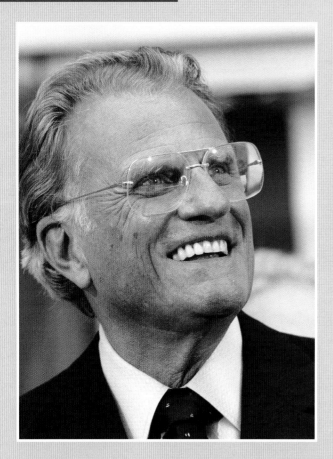

IN 1988, GEORGE W. BUSH WAS a good choice to reach out to conservative religious voters. In 1985, he had undergone a religious experience that changed his life. The Bushes had raised George W. in the Episcopal and Presbyterian Churches. Later, he attended Methodist church services with his wife, Laura. "I had always been a religious person," he once wrote, but "my faith took on a new meaning" after a weekend with the Reverend Billy Graham. Reverend Graham is one of the most famous Protestant ministers in the world. He often preaches in front of tens of thousands of people.

Graham gave Bush a new understanding of the Bible and Christian beliefs. Bush began to read the Bible regularly and discuss it with friends. Over time, Bush became a born-again Christian. His faith plays a very important role in his life.

Chapter THREE

From Governor to President

JUST AS THE PRESIDENT'S WIFE IS called the First Lady, George W. Bush was sometimes called the First Son. He had a close relationship with some of the president's advisers. He also worked hard for his father when he ran for president again in 1992. In that election, President Bush faced Democrat Bill Clinton. He also ran against Ross Perot, who had started his own party called the Reform Party.

George H. W. Bush greets U.S. troops in Saudi Arabia in 1990.

George H. W. Bush had been popular in 1991, after U.S. military forces helped remove invading Iraqi troops from Kuwait. But by the 1992 election, many voters questioned how the elder Bush had handled the U.S.

George W. Bush (right), broadcaster Joe Morgan (center), and George H. W. Bush (left) share a laugh in the Texas Rangers' locker room. Bush's role as part owner of the Texas Rangers made him a well-known figure in Texas.

economy. During part of his presidency, many workers had lost their jobs. The president had also broken a promise he made to not raise taxes. And the presence of a third presidential candidate hurt Bush. Some people who might have voted for the Republicans in the past decided to support Perot. In November, Bill Clinton was elected the 42nd president. George W. later called 1992 "a long and miserable year."

As the next year began, George W. planned to enter politics once again. In the fall, he announced he was running for governor of Texas. The current governor was Democrat Ann Richards, who was well liked by many people in the state. Some of Bush's advisers thought he could not win a campaign against the popular governor. Bush, however, was confident that he could win. More Texans now knew him because of his work with the Texas Rangers. And, as the son of a former

U.S. president, people knew the Bush family and what they believed in.

George W. was not always comfortable making speeches. He did best when he met voters in small groups. He talked about reducing crime and improving education. He also wanted to help the owners of small businesses. He called the people who ran their own companies "the backbone of our society." In November 1994, Bush easily defeated Richards.

Bush was only the second Republican governor of Texas in more than 120 years. He had to work closely with Democratic lawmakers. He was able to win their support many times. He cut taxes and toughened jail sentences for young criminals. He also reformed the **welfare system.** Bush wanted people who received government aid to find jobs or go to school so they could learn new skills. His goal was to get people off welfare.

In 1998, Bush faced a major issue that brought him national attention. He had often spoken about protecting citizens and keeping criminals in jail. He also supported the death penalty. A Texas woman named Karla Fay Tucker was scheduled to be executed for

▶ George W. was not the first Bush son to run for governor. Jeb Bush started campaigning in Florida just a few months before George W. entered the Texas race. Jeb lost his election, but in 1998 he ran again and won. He was reelected in 2002.

▶ As a candidate and politician, George W. Bush believed it was important to always be on time for public events. He usually arrived early—sometimes even before reporters and TV cameras reached the event. Bush's aides often told him to drive around the block so the reporters had time to prepare for his arrival.

Protestors gathered outside the prison where Karla Fay Tucker was held. Despite their protests, Tucker was executed in 1998.

killing two people. While in prison, Tucker had become a Christian. Some Christians wanted Bush to stop her execution.

As governor, he had the power to do so. Bush, however, said his first duty was to follow the laws as they were written. He believed strongly that because a jury had found Tucker guilty, she should receive the punishment called for by Texas law. People who opposed the death penalty criticized Bush for letting Tucker be executed.

Liberals in the Democratic Party also attacked many of his policies. They said he favored businesses over average citizens. But in the 1998 campaign for governor, many Democrats supported Bush and he easily won reelection.

After his victory, Bush said, "My compassionate conservative philosophy is making Texas a better place." Bush had been

calling himself a compassionate conservative for more than a year. That meant that he
held conservative views, such as limiting the
powers of the government, promoting business growth, and upholding the law when
people commit crimes. At the same time, he
also believed government should help people
when they truly needed it.

Even before Bush won his reelection,
he was thinking about running for president.
President Bill Clinton had won a second term
in 1996, and Vice President Al Gore was
the most likely Democrat to run for president in 2000. By 1999, Bush was meeting
with Republican Party advisers to learn more
about important issues. He also started raising
money. Running for president is expensive,
because candidates must travel across the
country and buy TV ads to communicate
their views. Bush eventually raised more than
$100 million for his campaign.

The major political parties choose
their candidates through **primaries.** Voters
in most states get to vote for the candidates
who want to run for president. In 2000, Bush
was one of several Republicans who wanted

Vice-presidential candidate Dick Cheney gives the crowd the thumbs-up sign at the 2000 Republican Convention.

to represent their party. For a time, Senator John McCain of Arizona was his toughest opponent. By mid-March, however, Bush had won nineteen state primaries to McCain's seven. McCain pulled out of the race, and gave his support to Bush.

Bush won the nomination, and chose Dick Cheney as his vice presidential candidate. As most people expected, Al Gore was the Democratic candidate for president.

During his campaign, Bush continued to spread his message of compassionate conservatism. He supported a new program that would give religious organizations a larger role in helping troubled people while shrinking the government's role. Bush also wanted to cut taxes and spend more money on the U.S. military. Bush hoped to end arguments between Republicans and Democrats. He pointed out that he worked well with Democrats in Texas. Bush told the nation,

"I am a uniter, not a divider."

The 2000 presidential election was one of the closest in U.S. history. On Election Day, Gore won more total votes, or the popular vote. Bush, however, won more electoral votes. In all but two states, the winner of the popular vote receives all the state's electoral votes. Each state has one electoral vote for each person it sends to Congress, which is based partly on the state's population.

In 2000, the final results were delayed for almost six weeks because of voting problems in Florida. When the results from that state finally came in, Bush won by just one electoral vote.

On January 20, 2001, George W. Bush was sworn in as the 43rd president of the United States. The nation looked on as he promised to preserve, protect, and defend the U.S. Constitution. Bush then said he would "pursue the public interest with courage." He also wanted to end the hostility between Republicans and Democrats, sparked by the close vote in Florida. He hoped members of both parties would "come together and do what's right for America."

EVEN BEFORE ELECTION DAY 2000 WAS OVER, SOME PEOPLE COMPLAINED about the voting process in Florida. Some voters found that their names were not on the list of legal voters. In some counties, new **ballots** confused voters, who ended up casting votes that didn't reflect their wishes.

The day ended with Bush ahead of Gore by just a few thousand votes. Under Florida law, the votes had to be recounted before state officials could declare a winner. After the recount, Florida's secretary of state, Katherine Harris (below) was responsible for declaring the winner. Democrats were upset because Harris was a Republican. And because the state's governor was Bush's brother Jeb, they worried about getting a fair count. But Harris, as an elected state official, was expected to make sure the recount was fair.

The recount process ended up in court, as both sides argued over which

ballots should be counted. In December, the legal battle went to the U.S. Supreme Court, the most powerful court in the country. Gore and the Democrats wanted more time for a recount of about 9,000 votes cast in a south Florida county. In their decision, the majority of the nine Supreme Court justices said the recount had to stop. They said it was unconstitutional to continue to count the votes in only one county, instead of the entire state. As a result, the original recount stood. Bush won the state by slightly more than 500 votes out of more than 6 million cast.

Chapter FOUR

A Time of War

As his presidency began, Bush focused on **domestic** issues. The U.S. economy had weakened, and some people were losing their jobs. As he had promised, Bush asked Congress to pass a huge tax cut, the first of three during the first term of his presidency. Bush's plan was to give taxpayers more money to save for the future. They could also spend the money, which would help companies that make products. Those companies could then hire more workers.

President Bush speaks to the American people about his first round of tax cuts.

Bush said, "My plan sets out to make life better for average men, women, and children." To help businesses further, he ended some government rules that cost companies money that could have been used to hire new workers.

Bush also looked at some international

U.S. warships equipped with missiles line up at sea in 2001. Protecting the United States is a top priority for President Bush.

issues. He called for a new missile defense system to protect the country. The system would shoot down enemy missiles in space, before they reached the United States. Under an old treaty with Russia, the United States was not supposed to build this new missile system. Bush argued that protecting America was more important than honoring the treaty.

He also pulled out of another treaty designed to limit air pollution. In 1997, the United States had agreed to limit the production of certain gases thought to harm the environment. Bush decided that following the treaty would be too costly for U.S. businesses, and that those costs would eventually be passed on to consumers as price increases.

Some of Bush's decisions angered Democrats. They thought Bush was breaking his promise to work with them and be a "uniter."

But many Democrats joined with him to try to improve U.S. schools. Bush called this effort No Child Left Behind. He wanted to give states more money to improve schools. Students would be tested regularly at different ages to make sure they had learned what they were supposed to by that grade. Parents could move their children to better schools if the overall test scores at their current schools were too low.

Education, taxes, and other issues are vital to the United States. But after September 11, 2001, George W. Bush had a new priority. The terrorist attacks of that day showed that Americans faced a dangerous enemy. Al-Qaeda had attacked without warning and targeted civilians.

Bush decided he would strike back at al-Qaeda. He would also send U.S. troops to battle any country that helped terrorists. Bush told the nation, "We go forward to defend freedom and all that is good and just in the world." Bush called his efforts "a war on terrorism." His plan included keeping terrorists out of America and cutting off their funding. He also wanted the country

▶ The terrorist attacks of September 11 were not limited to New York City. Members of al-Qaeda crashed another hijacked plane into the Pentagon. That huge building just outside of Washington, D.C., contains the offices of U.S. military leaders. A fourth plane went down in a field in Pennsylvania. Passengers onboard tried to take back control of the plane from the hijackers. The passengers reached the cockpit, but the plane crashed during their struggle with the hijackers.

to further strengthen the military. Bush later created the Department of Homeland Security to help prevent future terrorist attacks.

Al-Qaeda's leader is Osama bin Laden. He and his supporters belong to an extreme branch of Islam, a religion that was started in Saudi Arabia almost 1,500 years ago. Followers of Islam are called Muslims. Extremist Muslims are called fundamentalists. These Muslim fundamentalists oppose all other religions. They believe they have a duty to kill people who do not accept the Koran, Islam's holy book. They also believe a country's laws should be based on the Koran. Bin Laden shares these views with the Taliban, a group of men who were the political and religious leaders of Afghanistan at the time of the September 11, 2001, terrorist attacks.

Bush knew bin Laden was responsible for the attacks in America. He told the Taliban to arrest bin Laden or the United States would attack. The Taliban ignored Bush's demands, and in October 2001, U.S. planes streaked over Afghanistan. Military troops from other countries also joined the battle, as did Afghan forces that opposed the Taliban.

Within two months, the **allies** had forced the Taliban from power. Bin Laden, however, was still on the loose in the rugged mountains between Afghanistan and Pakistan.

President Bush next turned his attention to Iraq. Reports from spies, as well as Iraqis who had escaped from the country, said that Iraq's ruler, Saddam Hussein, had helped al-Qaeda. They also said that Hussein had **weapons of mass destruction (WMDs).** The president feared the Iraqis might give them to terrorists so they could be used against the United States.

Osama bin Laden was born in 1957. His father was one of the wealthiest men in Saudi Arabia.

Relations between the United States and Iraq had been bad since the Gulf War of 1991. Even before September 11, some of Bush's advisers thought the United States would have to remove Hussein from power to protect U.S. security.

Throughout 2002, Bush spoke to Americans and explained that attacking Iraq was a key part of the war on terror. Some Democrats, however, wanted the United Nations (UN) to finish searching for WMDs in Iraq. UN rules required that Saddam Hussein give up all of his WMDs. UN teams had already been searching there for a long time. Still, most Democrats in Congress gave Bush the authority to invade Iraq.

By February 2003, several nations were willing to help the United States fight Iraq. Many others offered other kinds of support. Together, these allies were called the Coalition of the Willing. In March, Bush told Hussein that he had 48 hours to leave the country. If he refused, the United States would attack. Hussein claimed, as he had before, that Iraq did not have WMDs. He said he would not step down.

On March 19, U.S. military forces started a war that U.S. leaders called Operation Iraqi Freedom. Within four weeks, the Americans and their allies had taken Baghdad, the Iraqi capital, and forced Saddam Hussein from power. On May 1, Bush said major fighting was over in Iraq. "We have removed an ally of al-Qaeda," he added, "and cut off a source of terrorist funding." The president warned it would take time to bring complete peace and **democracy** to Iraq.

In the months that followed, Iraqi insur-

President Bush boards the S3 Viking jet that will take him to the USS Abraham Lincoln. *After arriving on the ship, Bush announced an end to major combat in Iraq.*

gents, fighters opposed to the coalition, began to attack U.S. forces. Some foreign fighters also helped them battle the Americans. Most Iraqis, however, welcomed the U.S. forces and the end of Saddam Hussein's brutal rule.

In June 2004, the United States turned over control of the Iraqi government to Iraqis who supported democratic rule. However, insurgents continued to attack coalition troops, who remained in the country to help keep order.

Some Americans thought President Bush had not told the truth about Iraqi WMDs before the war started. Not all U.S. intelligence agencies agreed that Hussein had these weapons. Later, Bush argued that Hussein had to be removed even if he did not have WMDs. He had been a brutal ruler who often killed and tortured his own people.

In 2004, Bush ran for a second term as president. His popularity had fallen since September 2001. Some Americans questioned his decision to invade Iraq. Others did not like his tax cuts and believed the economy was suffering.

Bush argued that his policies would add new jobs in the years to come. He said he was the best person to lead the country's war on terror. "If America shows uncertainty and weakness in this decade," the president said, "the world will drift toward tragedy. This will not happen on my watch." Bush cited his leadership in the weeks following the 9/11 attacks, and in the war on terror.

Bush's opponent in 2004 was Senator John Kerry of Massachusetts. Kerry had won several medals during the Vietnam

War. During the campaign, he talked often about his war record. He said his experience would make him a good commander in chief. Yet he also believed in using **diplomacy.** He attacked Bush for not trying hard enough to avoid a war in Iraq although he had voted in favor of the 2002 joint resolution. Kerry and his Democratic supporters also promised to end some of Bush's tax cuts.

President George W. Bush and Senator John Kerry debate at the University of Miami on September 30, 2004.

In November 2004, U.S. voters chose George W. Bush over John Kerry. Unlike the 2000 election, Bush easily won the popular vote as well as the electoral count. The day after the election, Bush said he looked forward to helping democracy grow in Afghanistan and Iraq. He also wanted to strengthen the U.S. economy. And he thanked voters for their support. "I'm proud to lead such an amazing country," he said, "and I'm proud to lead it forward."

Interesting Fact

▶ Of the more than 115 million people who voted in the November 2004 presidential election, 51 percent voted for President Bush. It was the first time since 1988 that the winner received a true majority—more than 50 percent—of the popular vote.

THE UNITED STATES HAS HAD A LONG relationship with Saddam Hussein (right). He rose to power during the early 1970s. In 1980, he invaded neighboring Iran. In the eight-year war that followed, the United States gave Hussein military aid. U.S. leaders thought Iran was a bigger threat to U.S. interests than Iraq.

In 1991, however, President George H. W. Bush quickly acted to end Hussein's invasion of Kuwait. He led a coalition of countries to drive the Iraqis out of Kuwait. The Iraqi military surrendered quickly, and the Kuwaiti royal family was restored to rule. Some Americans discussed forcing Hussein from power during the Gulf War, but the first President Bush said no.

After the Gulf War, U.S. and British planes still flew over northern and southern Iraq. Their mission was to prevent Hussein from sending his military forces into those areas. Now Hussein saw the United States as his major enemy. At times, Iraqi soldiers shot at U.S. and British planes as they patrolled the skies. The Americans and British then attacked the Iraqis. Hussein also tried to **assassinate** George H. W. Bush after he left office. The plot failed. When President Bill Clinton learned of the plot, he ordered an attack on Iraqi targets in retaliation.

When Operation Iraqi Freedom began in March 2003, Saddam Hussein escaped from Baghdad. U.S. and coalition forces searched for him for months, sometimes coming within minutes of capturing him. Finally, in December 2003, an Iraqi citizen led U.S. forces to a farmhouse in the countryside. Saddam Hussein was found hiding in a **spider hole** there and captured.

1946 George W. Bush is born on July 6 in New Haven, Connecticut. His parents are George H. W. and Barbara Bush.

1948 The Bush family moves to Texas.

1964 Bush graduates from Phillips Academy in Massachusetts and helps his father during his campaign for the U.S. Senate.

1968 After graduating from Yale University, Bush enters the Texas Air National Guard and learns how to fly fighter jets.

1975 Bush graduates with a business degree from Harvard University.

1977 Over the summer, Bush meets Laura Welch, a school librarian. They marry in November.

1978 Bush loses his first political race, for a seat in the U.S. House of Representatives.

1979 Bush starts Arbusto Energy, which he later renames Bush Exploration.

1980 George H. W. Bush, Bush's father, is elected vice president of the United States. Ronald Reagan is elected president.

1988 During the presidential election, Bush helps run his father's campaign. In November, the elder Bush is elected the 41st president of the United States.

1989 Bush and some business partners buy the Texas Rangers baseball team.

1994 Bush defeats Democrat Ann Richards to become the second Republican governor of Texas in more than 120 years.

1998 Calling himself a compassionate conservative, Bush wins reelection as governor of Texas.

1999 Bush prepares to run for president in 2000.

2000 The Republican Party chooses Bush as its candidate for president. The Democrats nominate Vice President Al Gore. The race is close, and the final result is decided in Florida. After a recount of the votes, Bush wins Florida, and the presidency, by just over 500 votes. The result is later upheld by the U.S. Supreme Court.

2001 President Bush cuts taxes. On September 11, al-Qaeda terrorists strike the United States, killing almost 3,000 people. Bush immediately makes plans to hunt down Osama bin Laden, the leader of al-Qaeda, and remove the Taliban, the leaders of Afghanistan who support him. U.S. forces and their allies defeat the Taliban, but they do not find bin Laden.

2002 Bush calls for more money for the military to defend America against terrorist attacks. He also seeks more tax cuts to help boost the U.S. economy. The president and his advisers say Iraq's Saddam Hussein has weapons of mass destruction and could share them with terrorists. Congress gives the president the authority to send troops to Iraq if he thinks the safety of the United States is being threatened.

2003 President Bush assembles a group of nations, called the Coalition of the Willing, to support an invasion of Iraq. The largest military help comes from Great Britain. In March, U.S. forces begin Operation Iraqi Freedom, and within a month they control the government. Saddam Hussein flees but is later arrested. In May, Bush declares that major combat operations have ended.

2004 The United States gives back control of Iraq to the Iraqis, but more than 100,000 troops remain in the country. At home, Bush says the economy is strengthening, thanks partly to his tax cuts. Bush faces harsh criticism about the war in Iraq, but he defeats Democrat John Kerry in the 2004 presidential election and prepares to begin his second term as U.S. president.

allies (AL-eyez)
Allies are people or nations who unite for a common goal. President George W. Bush, convinced many allies to help fight wars in Afghanistan and Iraq.

ambassador (am-BASS-uh-dur)
An ambassador represents his or her country in dealings with foreign nations. During the early 1970s, George H. W. Bush served as the U.S. ambassador to the United Nations.

assassinate (uh-SASS-uh-nayt)
To kill government or business leaders for political reasons is to assassinate them. Saddam Hussein tried to assassinate George H. W. Bush in 1993.

ballots (BAL-uhts)
Ballots are the slips of paper or other items used to record votes in an election. During the 2000 presidential election, some ballots in Florida did not work properly.

campaign (kam-PAYN)
A campaign is the process of running for an election, including such activities as giving speeches and meeting voters. George W. Bush worked on his father's campaigns before he ran for office himself.

candidates (KAN-dih-dates)
Candidates are people running in an election. George W. Bush was the Republican candidate for president in 2000 and 2004. By law, he cannot run for president again.

coalition (KOH-uh-LISH-uhn)
A group of nations united to fight a common enemy forms a coalition. President George W. Bush created a coalition to defeat Iraq in 2003.

Communists (KOM-yuh-nists)
Communists support a government that owns all business and property and limits what citizens can do. U.S. leaders did not want Communists to take power in South Vietnam, so they fought the Vietnam War.

conservative (kuhn-SUR-vah-tiv)
A conservative believes the government should play a small role in the economy, grow national social programs more slowly, and build a strong defense. George W. Bush is hugely popular with conservative Americans.

democracy (dih-MOK-ruh-see)
A political system with free elections is called a democracy. The United States tried to bring democracy to Afghanistan and Iraq.

diplomacy (di-PLO-muh-see)
Diplomacy is the process of nations resolving differences in a peaceful way. In 2004, John Kerry said President Bush did not use enough diplomacy before going to war with Iraq.

domestic (duh-MESS-tik)
Events and issues linked to what happens within a nation are called domestic. When he began his first term as president, George W. Bush made tax cuts one of his most important domestic issues.

drafted (DRAF-ted)
When people are drafted, they are required by law to join the military. After college, George W. Bush joined the Texas Air National Guard and therefore was not affected by the draft.

hijacked (HI-jakt)
Something that is hijacked is taken by force. In 2001, terrorists hijacked four U.S. planes and crashed them, killing almost 3,000 people.

joint resolution (JOYNT res-uh-LOO-shun)
A joint resolution is a special vote held by the two branches of Congress, the House of Representatives and the U.S. Senate. In 2002, a joint resolution gave President Bush the power to invade Iraq.

leases (LEES-ez)
Leases are legal documents that detail how much money a person will pay to rent property or other items. In Texas, George W. Bush bought and sold leases dealing with oil.

legislature (LEJ-is-lay-chur)
The branch of government that makes laws is called the legislature. In 1972, George W. Bush thought about running for the Texas legislature but decided he needed more experience.

liberals (LIB-ur-uhlz)
Liberals are people who believe the government should play a large role in the economy, spend more money on social programs, and cut down on spending for national defense. Many liberals attacked Bush's policies while he was governor of Texas. Many liberals opposed George W. Bush's decision to invade Iraq.

nomination (nom-ih-NAY-shun)
If someone receives a nomination, he or she is chosen by a political party to run for an office. In 2000, Senator John McCain was George W. Bush's main opponent for the Republican presidential nomination.

primaries (PRY-mar-eez)
The elections held by political parties to choose candidates are called primaries. George W. Bush won enough votes in the 2000 Republican primaries to become his party's candidate for president.

spider hole (SPY-duhr HOLE)
A spider hole is a round hole dug deep into the ground that is used as protection or as a hiding place. Saddam Hussein was pulled from a spider hole that was covered by a rug to hide the opening.

terrorist (TAIR-uhr-ist)
A terrorist is a person who uses violence and fear to force others to do something. On September 11, 2001, terrorists hijacked four planes and killed almost 3,000 people.

United Nations (yoo-NYE-tid NAY-shunz)
The United Nations was formed in 1945 to try to keep peace around the world. During the 1990s, the United Nations destroyed many of Iraq's weapons of mass destruction.

weapons of mass destruction (WMDs) (WEP-uhns OV MASS di-STRUK-shun)
Devices that can kill thousands of people at once are called weapons of mass destruction. In 2002, President George W. Bush feared Iraq would give WMDs to terrorists.

welfare system (WEL-fair SIS-tuhm)
Government programs that help the poor, sick, and elderly are called the welfare system. Bush supports reducing funds for the welfare system.

Our PRESIDENTS

President	Birthplace	Life Dates	Term	Political Party	First Lady
George Washington	Virginia	1732–1799	1789–1797	None	Martha Dandridge Custis Washington
John Adams	Massachusetts	1735–1826	1797–1801	Federalist	Abigail Smith Adams
Thomas Jefferson	Virginia	1743–1826	1801–1809	Democratic-Republican	widower
James Madison	Virginia	1751–1836	1809–1817	Democratic-Republican	Dolley Payne Todd Madison
James Monroe	Virginia	1758–1831	1817–1825	Democratic-Republican	Elizabeth "Eliza" Kortright Monroe
John Quincy Adams	Massachusetts	1767–1848	1825–1829	Democratic-Republican	Louisa Catherine Johnson Adams
Andrew Jackson	South Carolina	1767–1845	1829–1837	Democrat	widower
Martin Van Buren	New York	1782–1862	1837–1841	Democrat	widower
William Henry Harrison	Virginia	1773–1841	1841	Whig	Anna Tuthill Symmes Harrison
John Tyler	Virginia	1790–1862	1841–1845	Whig	Letitia Christian Tyler Julia Gardiner Tyler
James Polk	North Carolina	1795–1849	1845–1849	Democrat	Sarah Childress Polk

42

Our PRESIDENTS

President	Birthplace	Life Dates	Term	Political Party	First Lady
Zachary Taylor	Virginia	1784–1850	1849–1850	Whig	Margaret Mackall Smith Taylor
Millard Fillmore	New York	1800–1874	1850–1853	Whig	Abigail Powers Fillmore
Franklin Pierce	New Hampshire	1804–1869	1853–1857	Democrat	Jane Means Appleton Pierce
James Buchanan	Pennsylvania	1791–1868	1857–1861	Democrat	never married
Abraham Lincoln	Kentucky	1809–1865	1861–1865	Republican	Mary Todd Lincoln
Andrew Johnson	North Carolina	1808–1875	1865–1869	Democrat	Eliza McCardle Johnson
Ulysses S. Grant	Ohio	1822–1885	1869–1877	Republican	Julia Dent Grant
Rutherford B. Hayes	Ohio	1822–1893	1877–1881	Republican	Lucy Ware Webb Hayes
James A. Garfield	Ohio	1831–1881	1881	Republican	Lucretia Rudolph Garfield
Chester A. Arthur	Vermont	1829–1886	1881–1885	Republican	widower
Grover Cleveland	New Jersey	1837–1908	1885–1889	Democrat	Frances Folsom Cleveland

43

Our PRESIDENTS

President	Birthplace	Life Dates	Term	Political Party	First Lady
Benjamin Harrison	Ohio	1833–1901	1889–1893	Republican	Caroline Lavina Scott Harrison
Grover Cleveland	New Jersey	1837–1908	1893–1897	Democrat	Frances Folsom Cleveland
William McKinley	Ohio	1843–1901	1897–1901	Republican	Ida Saxton McKinley
Theodore Roosevelt	New York	1858–1919	1901–1909	Republican	Edith Kermit Carow Roosevelt
William Howard Taft	Ohio	1857–1930	1909–1913	Republican	Helen Herron Taft
Woodrow Wilson	Virginia	1856–1924	1913–1921	Democrat	Ellen L. Axson Wilson Edith Bolling Galt Wilson
Warren G. Harding	Ohio	1865–1923	1921–1923	Republican	Florence Kling De Wolfe Harding
Calvin Coolidge	Vermont	1872–1933	1923–1929	Republican	Grace Anna Goodhue Coolidge
Herbert Hoover	Iowa	1874–1964	1929–1933	Republican	Lou Henry Hoover
Franklin D. Roosevelt	New York	1882–1945	1933–1945	Democrat	Anna Eleanor Roosevelt Roosevelt
Harry S. Truman	Missouri	1884–1972	1945–1953	Democrat	Elizabeth "Bess" Virginia Wallace Truman

Our PRESIDENTS

President	Birthplace	Life Dates	Term	Political Party	First Lady
Dwight D. Eisenhower	Texas	1890–1969	1953–1961	Republican	Mamie Geneva Doud Eisenhower
John F. Kennedy	Massachusetts	1917–1963	1961–1963	Democrat	Jacqueline Lee Bouvier Kennedy
Lyndon Baines Johnson	Texas	1908–1973	1963–1969	Democrat	Claudia "Lady Bird" Alta Taylor Johnson
Richard M. Nixon	California	1913–1994	1969–1974	Republican	Thelma "Pat" Catherine Patricia Ryan Nixon
Gerald R. Ford	Nebraska	1913–	1974–1977	Republican	Elizabeth "Betty" Bloomer Warren Ford
James Earl Carter	Georgia	1924–	1977–1981	Democrat	Rosalynn Smith Carter
 Ronald Reagan	Illinois	1911–2004	1981–1989	Republican	Nancy Davis Reagan
George Bush	Massachusetts	1924–	1989–1993	Republican	Barbara Pierce Bush
William J. Clinton	Arkansas	1946–	1993–2001	Democrat	Hillary Rodham Clinton
George W. Bush	Connecticut	1946–	2001–	Republican	Laura Welch Bush

Presidential FACTS

Qualifications

To run for president, a candidate must
- be at least 35 years old
- be a citizen who was born in the United States
- have lived in the United States for 14 years

Term of Office

A president's term of office is four years. No president can stay in office for more than two terms.

Election Date

The presidential election takes place every four years on the first Tuesday of November.

Inauguration Date

Presidents are inaugurated on January 20.

Oath of Office

I do solemnly swear I will faithfully execute the office of the President of the United States and will to the best of my ability preserve, protect, and defend the Constitution of the United States.

Write a Letter to the President

One of the best things about being a U.S. citizen is that Americans get to participate in their government. They can speak out if they feel government leaders aren't doing their jobs. They can also praise leaders who are going the extra mile. Do you have something you'd like the president to do? Should the president worry more about the environment and encourage people to recycle? Should the government spend more money on our schools? You can write a letter to the president to say how you feel!

1600 Pennsylvania Avenue
Washington DC 20500

You can even send an e-mail to: president@whitehouse.gov

For Further INFORMATION

Internet Sites

Visit our home page for lots of links about George W. Bush:
http://www.childsworld.com/links.html

Note to Parents, Teachers, and Librarians: We routinely check our Web links to make sure they're safe, active sites—so encourage your readers to check them out!

Books

Francis, Sandra. *George Bush: Our Forty-First President.* Chanhassen, Minn.: The Child's World, 2002.

Gormley, Beatrice. *Laura Bush: America's First Lady.* New York: Aladdin Paperbacks, 2003.

Innes, Brian. *International Terrorism.* Broomall, Penn.: Mason Crest Publishers, 2003.

Jones, Veda Boyd. *George W. Bush.* Philadelphia: Chelsea House, 2003.

Landau, Elaine. *Friendly Foes: A Look at Political Parties.* Minneapolis: Lerner Publishing Company, 2004.

Richie, Jason. *Iraq and the Fall of Saddam Hussein.* Minneapolis: Oliver Press, 2003.